The Pearl of the Gospel

The Pearl of the Gospel

Short Reflections on Reciprocal Love

CHIARA LUBICH

Compiled and with a Foreword
by
Bill Hartnett

NEW CITY PRESS
of the Focolare
Hyde Park, NY

Published in the United States by New City Press
202 Comforter Blvd., Hyde Park, NY 12538
www.newcitypress.com
©2013 New City Press of the Focolare

Cover design by Leandro de Leon

Bible citations unless otherwise noted are from the *New Revised Standard Version Bible*, copyright 1989, Division of Christian Education of the National Council of the Churches of Christ in the United States of America.

A catalog record is available from the Library of Congress.

ISBN: 978-1-56548-495-5

Printed in the United States of America

Contents

Foreword. 7

Short Reflections on
    Reciprocal Love 15

Notes 79

For Further Reading 86

Foreword

Jesus' new commandment is one of the cardinal points of the Focolare spirituality. Chiara Lubich came to appreciate this new commandment during a dramatic moment in her life. She and some of her early companions had been pondering whether, before they might perish in their war-torn city of Trent, there was something special they could do for God, a specific action that would be particularly pleasing to him. One day, during a heavy bombardment, Chiara and her friends were unable to reach an air-raid shelter so they took refuge in the cellar beneath a house. As bombs rained down, they again asked if there were something that they could do in that moment, which could be their last. Their hearts burning with love for God, Chiara says, they wanted to spend their last moments loving him in the best way possible.

They opened their small copy of the gospels at random to this passage: "I give you a new commandment, that you love one another. Just as I have loved you, you also should love one another" (Jn 13:34). Up until that moment they had been trying to live out the two great commandments: "You shall love the Lord your God with all your heart, and with all your soul, and with all your mind," and "You shall love your neighbor as yourself" (see Mt 22:36–40). Right then, Chiara noted, the Lord revealed to them a "new" commandment that he called "his." At that dramatic moment, they looked at each other and said: "Then it will be our commandment too." Out of love for God, whom they wanted to love above all things, they solemnly declared their willingness to die for each other.

There were three wondrous gifts that Jesus had "held hidden in his heart," to be revealed only on the last day of his life on earth: the Eucharist, the gift of his body, blood, soul, and divinity; the ministerial priesthood (which Chiara sees as a vocation to pure service toward brothers and sisters, demonstrated in Jesus' washing the feet of the apostles); and his "own" "new" commandment. It was a discovery that changed everything; beyond it there was nothing newer. Chiara recognized that these three gifts were equally new but found something completely unprecedented in the new commandment, which she suggests had been "forgotten" by Christians. For Chiara the great discovery here, what is truly new, emerges from the words "as I have loved you" and in the fact that Jesus commands that this love be mutual.

The long period of mystical experiences that has come to be known as "Paradise of '49" began one particular day during Chiara's reception of Holy Communion. She had agreed with her companions to ask Jesus in the Eucharist to negotiate the unity among them as he wanted it to be. Afterwards, however, as she turned to Jesus in prayer, she could not utter his name. Another came to her lips: "Abba!", "Father." Somehow, she and that small group with whom she was striving to live the new commandment had come to share the same identity with Jesus. This transformation was related to their practice of living the Word, especially the new commandment and its key words that express the measure of Jesus' love: "as I have loved you." In his abandonment on the cross he "emptied himself" and "became nothing." He became one with human beings and made us one with God. At that moment in 1949, Jesus in the Eucharist had brought about the miracle of unity in their small community. They had become a "living cell" of the Mystical Body of Christ. They were "with Jesus" "in the bosom of the Father, turned toward the Father with him, their Brother."

Although the Word of God, the Eucharist, and the new commandment are ancient realities, Chiara's rediscovery of the new commandment has brought to the church a new form of spiritual life, which she has called a "collective spirituality," a "communitarian spirituality," a "spirituality of communion." In this spiritual life individuals go to God together with others. Therein lies another innovation. Those who live out this spirituality place the new commandment before every other norm or rule, even before the most "sacred" things. Chiara understood that the new commandment transcends merely living in harmony with one another as brothers and sisters. It is that, but much more. It is living out the self-emptying love conveyed by the words "as I have loved you." It means taking on each other's sorrows and joys just like Jesus who, though he never sinned, took upon himself every person's joys, their sorrows, their sins, and their hell. They become empty in order to be able to make themselves one with their neighbors, with God in their neighbor. And they do this not only as individuals, but as a community as well.

Chiara points out that this is the love that Jesus brought from his heavenly home. For her, life in Christ through mutual love is at the same time united and distinct, as it is in the Trinity. Jesus wants to live in us not only as individuals but in communion. Remaining in the world in his individuality would not have been enough for him, Chiara suggested in 1949, "even though he was God." Already God in and of himself, he lived in communion with the Father and the Holy Spirit. Therefore, through the great gifts that "poured from his heart" on Holy Thursday night he draws us into the Trinitarian life, a community, making us one in him and with each other as a "living cell" of his Mystical Body, the church. Thus Jesus gives witness to himself, a witness that the world is waiting to see.

One person continues in every moment to live perfectly the "as I have loved you" — Mary. As she stood beneath her Son's cross, her own loving-suffering united with his loving-suffering, she lived these words completely. She experienced her own abandonment by God when her Son, who was God, gave her to another (see Jn 19:26). As the Mother whom Jesus gave to us, she continues to extend her hand to everyone, inviting us to "draw near to her heart" where we "will find this love too." She will teach us how it is to be shared.

At times Chiara has referred to the new commandment as "the pearl" of the gospel. A pearl begins with a tiny grain of sand slipping inside an oyster's shell, causing a bit of irritation that is relieved by a protective coating. Then the oyster probably "forgets" it. But the patient pearl lies hidden, growing until it is "rediscovered" by some lucky diver who keeps it as a precious treasure. In Medieval times pearls were considered most precious because of their perfection and uniqueness. Perhaps the same could be said of the new commandment. It can be uncomfortable to talk about "mutual love." It can be even more irritating to practice "dying for one another." But Chiara urges us to declare "openly" our decision to love one another with a "pact of mutual love." Of course, Chiara suggests, it's not something to be done lightly and does require some kind of preparation. Such love is not mere sentiment, but the love of Jesus: "as I have loved you." But once we summon the courage to take that step — "each person in his or her own way," — we too will discover the pearl of the gospel, the unique and most precious treasure of our life. It will be most pleasing to God and bring the life of God among us, allowing us to carry out God's greatest pleasure.

Bill Hartnett

Short Reflections on Reciprocal Love

"I give you a new commandment,
that you love one another.
Just as I have loved you,
you also should love one another" (Jn 13:34).
He called this command his own and new.[1]

~

Until we discovered
the new commandment,
he had urged us
to love others.
But now we had to turn our attention
to each other and love as he loves,
giving our lives for each other.[2]

~

Love is
loving and being loved.
It's the Trinity.
Then God in you
will take up your hearts into his,
igniting the Trinity

within you,
who had been dwelling there perhaps
through grace,
but not active.[3]

~

*Y*ou cannot light up a space
— even if electricity is available —
until the current's two poles
are brought together.
The life of God in us is similar.
It must circulate in order to radiate
outside of us and give witness to Christ,
the One who links heaven to earth,
and people with one another.[4]

~

*S*o taken by her Jesus,
Mary reminds us
that his new commandment
is particularly dear to him,
because it's *his* and it is *new*.[5]

Place yourself at the service of all,
for this is service to God.
Then your neighbor will come to you
and will love you.
For in fraternal love
lies the fulfillment
of God's every desire.
And it is expressed in a command:
"... love one another.
Just as I have loved you,
you also should love one another" (Jn 13:34).[6]

~

Love is a fire
that spreads through our hearts
producing a perfect fusion.
Then you no longer find
you in you,
or your neighbor in you,
but Love,
the living God in you.[7]

~

To love
it is not necessary
to make a lot of noise:
love is dying to ourselves
and death is silence
and life in God
and God is the silence that speaks.[8]

⁓

Our unity in mutual love
should be
more and more constant,
more and more perfect.
In this love we experience
how God pours out his
Love wherever he finds
nothingness,
in the spirituality of the saints
based on self-denial
and the greatness of Mary,
the humblest of the Lord's servants.[9]

⁓

"I desire only God!"
But loving Him means
doing what he desires: mutual love.
Loving Him means
loving one another
with a practical,
effective, delicate,
and affectionate love.[10]

~

Jesus had given many commands,
spoken many words.
But Jesus had one command
that was all *his:*
"This is my commandment:
that you love one another
as I have loved you" (Jn 15:12).[11]

~

We wanted to love God
as he wanted to be loved.
We wanted to be like Him.
And so *our* duty and

our purpose most especially were
to love one another
as he had loved us.[12]

∽

"Above all, maintain constant love
for one another…" (1 Pt 4:8).
Let us never take a step
unless we are all united
by mutual love.[13]

∽

The strength
that came from the union
brought about by mutual love
soon prompted us
to reflect on Jesus' words:
"For where two or three
are gathered in my name,
I am there among them" (Mt 18:20).[14]

∽

Mutual love
  isn't sentimentalism.
  It's a continual sacrifice
  of one's self
  in order to live the life
  of one's neighbor.[15]

~

Mutual love
  is perfect self-denial
  (see Mt 16:24).[16]

~

"Bear one another's burdens,
and in this way you will fulfill
the law of Christ" (Gal 6:2).
Mutual love
means carrying
each other's burdens.[17]

Mutual love
means sharing everything
with our neighbor
— both what is spiritual and
what is material —
as Jesus gave himself to us, completely,
on the Cross and in the Eucharist,
Body, Blood, Soul, and Divinity.[18]

∼

"That they may all be one.
As you, Father, are in me and I am in you,
may they also be in us,
so that the world may believe
that you have sent me" (Jn 17:21).
In perfect mutual love,
we realized
that we were living Jesus' final request
of his Father.
It was our rule of life,
the gospel summed up.[19]

∼

If the measure of our mutual love
is death on a cross,
then anything else
we should do
for one another
is really precious little! [20]

~

Give yourself
to every neighbor
in order to give yourself
to Jesus.
And Jesus will give himself to you.
It's love's law:
"Give and it will be given to you" (Lk 6:38). [21]

~

Through mutual love
we are drawn into unity.
Then, in this unity,
our brother and sister
is our penance, our mortification,

because loving them
requires putting our ego
to death.[22]

~

Allow yourself
to be possessed by your neighbor
— out of love for Jesus —
to be "eaten" by your neighbor
like another Eucharist.[23]

~

Being one with our neighbor
means forgetting ourselves
utterly and forever.[24]

~

If we're willing
to give our lives
for each other,
it's only logical

that in the meantime
we respond
to the thousands of demands
that loving like a brother or sister
places on us:
sharing joys, sorrows,
a few possessions,
spiritual experiences.[25]

~

Mutual love
requires us to set aside everything,
even our own souls,
in order to live the joys and sorrows
of our neighbors,
in order to demonstrate our love
to Jesus,
being crucified with Him
who lives in our neighbor
and, in his company,
rediscovering our happiness.[26]

~

Before going to Mass
or Holy Communion,
we would ask each other:
"Are we ready to give our lives
for each other?"
Because the Gospel advises:
"So when you are offering your gift
at the altar,
if you remember that your brother or sister
has something against you,
leave your gift there
before the altar and go;
first be reconciled to your brother or sister,
and then come and offer your gift"
(Mt 5:23–24).[27]

~

Mutual love
means living your neighbor,
so as to live Christ
crucified in your neighbor.
Just as Jesus who, by becoming man,
took upon himself
all our sins,
all our pain.[28]

Each morning
we would sit in a circle
— the eight of us girls —
and looking at everyone,
each of us would say:
"I am ready to die for you."
"I for you." "I for you."
All of us for each one of us.
We had begun a new lifestyle,
in the style of the new commandment.[29]

The pact,
the agreement
to love one another
even to the point of dying
for one another.
What a solemn pact.
It's the foundation upon which
the entire Work of Mary rests,
and it's the heart
of the Christian message.[30]

From the earliest days
of the Focolare,
looking to our model
Jesus crucified and Forsaken
(this is our measure, the "as"),
we understood that faithfulness
to mutual love
would bring about unity
according to the life of the Trinity.[31]

~

I was so struck by some words
written about the early Christians:
"Look! How they love each other,
each of them is ready to die for the other"
(Tertullian, *Apologetico* 39:7).
May people *see* our love
for each other,
not for the sake of our vanity
but in order to guarantee
that we're giving witness.
Let's stoke up the heat
of our mutual charity."[32]

*O*bviously,
  we're not always asked
  to give up our physical lives
  for our brothers and sisters.
  But spiritually, yes,
  and this is done by forgetting ourselves,
  denying ourselves
  in order to make ourselves
  one with them,
  to "live them"
  in order to serve them adequately.[33]

*I*f we observe what the Holy Spirit
  has always taught us,
  we will see that there is
  a martyrdom that's typically ours:
  it's the one entailed in the
  mutual love that Jesus asks of us.[34]

Oh, if only Jesus could
  see his testament
  fulfilled on earth,
  at least among us.[35]

∾

If I had to leave this world today,
  I'd let Jesus in me repeat to you:
  Love one another…
  until all are one.[36]

∾

Mutual love
  is a true martyrdom.
  It makes us authentic Christians.
  We reach perfection,
  as did the martyrs.
  And with martyrdom,
  union with God,
  the fullness of Christ's presence
  in us.
  Let's get to it then!

Let's renew, perfect,
make our mutual love shine,
give it the measure of our lives.[37]

~

*R*emember what Scripture says:
"*Ante omnia* — above all —
maintain constant love
for one another" (see 1 Pt 4:8).
Before everything then
before studying, before working,
before praying, before sleeping,
before eating, before our own life, before
anything that's in our heart,
before all things:
constant mutual love.[38]

~

*W*e should look at one another
and begin to love one another
in order to accomplish this will of God
that is so specifically
Jesus' own.[39]

From the moment we begin
to live the new commandment seriously,
there's a new joy, a new strength,
a burning desire to do good,
and a light that seems to pervade
us entirely.
What's happening?
We're experiencing what Jesus promises:
"For where two or three are gathered
in my name, I am there among them"
(Mt 18:20).[40]

~

When we live the new commandment,
the something wonderfully new
that we feel in our hearts is the effect
of his presence
among us.[41]

~

The new commandment
asks us to love each other
to the point of giving our lives

one for the other.
And this is martyrdom,
bloodless martyrdom, if you like,
but real martyrdom,
because it asks you
for your life.[42]

∽

"As I have loved you."
He loved us
to the point of the Abandonment.
In that moment
he took upon himself
all our darkness,
all our sins.
He made himself
one with us.
He made us one with God.
And we should
love one another
as he has loved us.
This is the love
that leads to Unity.[43]

∽

The new commandment
is very demanding, yes,
but don't be frightened.
Others have gone before you:
Jesus, Mary,
the saints, and many
beautiful souls.[44]

~

Only love counts.
And so we are willing
to feel like sin
with a brother or sister who sins,
like error with a brother or sister who errs,
like excommunication with a
brother or sister who is excommunicated[45]

~

After having said
that God has loved us,
St. John does not draw
what would seem the more

logical conclusion:
that we in turn should love God.
Instead he says,
"Beloved, since God loved us so much,
we also ought to love one another"
(1 Jn 4:11).[46]

~

May we lead the life
that Jesus led,
continuing it in our own lives.
He made himself
one with us
in order to bring us to the Father.[47]

~

He became darkness with us,
in order to give us the Light.
He became sin with us,
sorrow and death with us,
in order to give us the Life.
And so should it be for us.
In contact with any neighbor,

we should become what that neighbor is,
so that, as with Jesus,
our neighbor can become what we are;
that is, our neighbor may possess
the fullness of joy that comes
from mutual love
in a community
with Jesus in its midst.[48]

∼

Mary is *the* model of mutual love.
Our Lady did her share.
In order to love according to mutual love,
you need to love according
to the measure of Jesus:
"As I have loved you."
At the foot of the Cross
Mary arrived at this measure.
In her desolation
she lived the abandonment.
In losing Jesus,
in some way,
she lost God.[49]

When the Word of God
became a human being,
he certainly adapted himself
to earthly life.
He was a boy, a son,
a man, and a worker,
but he brought with him
a way of living that was proper to
his own Heavenly homeland.
He wanted people and things
to be recomposed according to
this new order,
according to the law of Heaven:
mutual love.[50]

When we are united
in mutual love
Christ is among us,
Head of the Mystical Body.
Here he continues to suffer
within himself
the sorrows of each brother,
each sister,

continuing the Passion
and the Redemption,
continuing to be the cause of Life
in each and every human being
who comes into contact
with us.[51]

∽

How many conversions
when we love one another
as he has loved us![52]

∽

"By this everyone will know
that you are my disciples
if you have love
for one another" (Jn 13:35).
This new way of life
based on the new commandment
witnesses Christ to the world.
Yes, because the new commandment
fulfills his promise:
"For where two or three

are gathered in my name,
I am there among them"
(Mt 18:20).[53]

~

Look upon every neighbor
from the standpoint of love
by loving them.
But one gift calls for another,
and you'll be loved in return.[54]

~

Because of the
agape love
that has been poured
into our hearts,
Christian love
is radically new
and belongs to the
new era.
And the commandment
is radically new,
introducing an utterly new

ethic into the human story:
love for one's enemy,
giving one's life for one's sisters
and brothers.[55]

~

It is said
that when the first Christian communities
asked St. John
to speak about Jesus,
the aged apostle would only respond:
"Love one another, love
one another...."
Therefore, we Christians today
should always take to heart
and live Jesus' new commandment
even more deeply.[56]

~

The new commandment
is the most important thing
in your life.[57]

The new commandment
is our vocation.
It's the command that Jesus
called "his own".
And he said it was "new"
in order to underscore the
importance he gave to it.
Indeed, the first Christians,
in the writings of John,
considered it to be
the message *par excellence.*[58]

∼

"Owe no one anything,
except to love one another" (Rom 13:8).
The new commandment
is a call to us:
a call to love always,
to be prepared each day
to pay up what we owe,
our debts of love
toward each other.[59]

∼

Having been freed by the Spirit
who dwells in each one of us,
we are led by that same Spirit
who pours love into our hearts,
to love one another,
that each love the other, serve,
and is a slave to the other.[60]

Holy Thursday,
the day of a new commandment,
the Eucharist, priesthood,
and service.
What infinite treasures
Jesus reserved
for the last day of his life
on this earth.[61]

"My command is this:
love each other as I have loved you."
Lord, you have chosen us

for this path so dear to your heart.
Help us to follow it well
every day, until the end.[62]

~

The command
given to us yesterday,
on Holy Thursday,
at the final moment,
must truly be the pearl
that Jesus was saving in his heart
so that he could give it to us
at the last moment.[63]

~

Holy Thursday!
What treasures
pour from the Heart of Jesus!
How can we ever thank Him?
At least we can live the gifts:
His new commandment,
the Eucharist, Unity…
And let us not waste time!

Let's begin immediately,
right from this moment.[64]

∼

It is because of
the commandment
of mutual love
that our Ideal seems
something so new,
a commandment that urges us,
each time it is proclaimed,
to convert again,
so that we can become
what Jesus wants us to be.[65]

∼

Jesus instituted the Eucharist
and the ministerial priesthood
so that his new commandment
could become a reality in us,
and the life of the Trinity
could come down among
the members of his Mystical Body.[66]

God is Love
and since he is Love,
he is Trinity.
God is mutual love:
God is our *model*
of mutual love.[67]

Love of neighbor
is the way that leads
to mutual love.[68]

Unity is the *effect*
of mutual love.[69]

Jesus in the midst
is the *fruit*
of mutual love.[70]

Jesus Forsaken
is the *means*
for mutual love.[71]

∽

Eucharistic Jesus
is the *bond* of unity.[72]

∽

The Church
is the *environment*
of mutual love.[73]

∽

The Word of God
is essential
for a mutual love
that's divine,
distilled,
as God imagines it.

Without humility,
without patience,
there is no real love.[74]

The Holy Spirit
is the *expression*
of mutual love
in God.
When we live mutual love
he bestows all His Gifts
on us.[75]

I have the feeling
that mutual love is
the valid currency
for our present times.
Anyone
using a different currency
is using outdated money,
from another time.[76]

I'm fixated
on mutual love,
fixated.
But I think
this fixation comes
from the Holy Spirit:
"Aim for this! It puts to death
the old self in so many.
This is how
you will renew the Church,
its structures will be remade."
And so I'll speak of it
over and over again,
until I see Christians shining
like enamel — all glowing!"

~

We know
that Jesus took the place
that the Old Testament Law had occupied.
And so what is the will of God
that Jesus manifests?
What is the Law now?
It is summed up

in a new commandment.
And so living the will of God
is, above all,
living that command,
which has to be the basis
of every Christian's life.[78]

∽

We should declare openly
our willingness
to live the new commandment.
And this declaration
of mutual love
is sacred,
a sacred pact.
Even though it's so simple,
it's not easy.[79]

∽

When our hearts are united
and made One by Love,
then Love will reach out
to love others.

For with an eye that is simple,
Love will find itself in them
until all are one.[80]

~

We should certainly
carry out the will of God
in the present moment
with all our heart,
soul, and strength,
but within an air
of mutual love, an environment
under the influence of Jesus'
new commandment.[81]

~

Everything should be based
on mutual love. This is what
Jesus wants of us.[82]

~

Jesus' new commandment
brings us into direct contact
with divine inspiration.
It fascinates and draws us.
We find that it always seems new.
Living it makes us feel
in our element.[83]

∼

The new commandment
has always been such an important matter
for us smallest children of the Church.
It was also important for the Church
at its beginnings: "For this is the message
that you have heard from the beginning,
that we should love one another" (1 Jn 3:11).
It should still be of major importance
for today's Church as well.[84]

∼

The basic rule,
the norm
that alone gives value

to every other norm
and without which nothing has value
— neither prayer nor apostolate,
neither giving away our possessions
nor giving our lives —
is the presence of Jesus in our midst
through mutual love.[85]

∼

Jesus came down from Heaven.
He brought his way of thinking,
the life of his environment:
Heaven.
There above,
you love God
in a harmony of souls
that is unspeakably beautiful.
You love everyone
and are loved by everyone
in a Unity that is the perfection
of joy.[86]

∼

*O*nce,
when we were scarcely
protected from the bombs,
we wondered if there
was a will of God
that was particularly pleasing
to the heart of Jesus,
because our hearts were on fire
for God
and we wanted to live
our final moments
in the best way possible.
We opened the Gospel
and read: "This is my commandment,
that you love one another
as I have loved you.
No one has greater love than this,
to lay down one's life
for one's friends"
(Jn 15:12–13).
And so,
out of love for Jesus,
for love of God,
we said:
This will be *our* commandment.[87]

"All mine are yours,
and yours are mine" (Jn 17:10).
This is how inter-Trinitarian life works.
It is unconditional and mutual
giving and receiving.
It's total and eternal communion
between Father and Son in the Spirit[88]

∼

Mutual love
is what most characterizes
Christians,
because mutual love
is what most characterizes
the Most Holy Trinity.[89]

∼

The Most Holy Trinity
is made like this:
each Person loves
the other, is loved in return,
and the Holy Spirit proceeds…

Therefore, people like us,
whose system of belief accepts that
God is Triune,
immediately understand
that what is most specific to this belief
is mutual love.[90]

~

Jesus was not content
with simply underlining
and linking to one another
the two fundamental commandments
of the Old Testament: "You shall love the
Lord, your God,
with all your heart, with all your soul,
and with all your mind….
You shall love your neighbor
as yourself" (Mt 22:37–39).
Instead, he teaches us
the commandment which he himself
does not hesitate to call "his" and "new,"
and by means of which
we can live the life of the Trinity

here on earth:
"Love one another
as I have loved you" (see Jn 13:34; 15:12).[91]

∼

"Let us make humankind in our own image,
according to our likeness" (Gn 1:26)
Humankind cannot be
but in the image of God,
of the One and Triune God.[92]

∼

The commandment of mutual love
lived according to the example of
Jesus' love for us,
to the point of forsakenness
that makes us one in him,
defines the very vision of humankind
that Jesus reveals to us
and that is the heart
of Christian anthropology.[93]

∼

We should love
one another
to the point of being consumed in one.
Just as God who,
being Love,
is Trinity
and Unity.[94]

∽

Jesus
brought
the actual life of Heaven
to earth.
It's the life
of the Most Holy Trinity
that we must emulate,
loving one another,
with the help of God's grace,
as the Persons of the
Most Holy Trinity love one another.[95]

∽

When you live the new commandment,
striving to welcome the Father's gift
of unity in Jesus,
the life of the Trinity is no longer lived
only in the inner life
of the individual but
flows freely
among the members of the
Mystical Body of Christ.[96]

~

Recently,
we understood more deeply
that we have to die in earnest
for each sister and brother,
not with the shedding of blood,
but with our souls, losing
everything, everything, everything,
in order to enter into them,
to embrace their sufferings,
their pains…they doing the same for us.
Mutual love is:
"Love one another *as* I have
loved you."

Jesus loved us to the point
of being totally abandoned,
and so must we live Jesus Forsaken,
and become nothingness
in order to enter into
the other.⁹⁷

~

The new commandment
wasn't so much a norm,
a precept, or a rule
that was added
to the ones we already knew,
as it was a way of living,
a fundamental approach to life
that we Christians had forgotten about.⁹⁸

~

What distinguished
the first Christians from others?
Was it their great works,
deep study,
polished eloquence?

Was it perhaps their miracles
or ecstasy?
No, no, no, no:
it was love,
their love for each other.
"Look! See how they love
one another. Each of them
is ready to die for the other"
(Tertullian, *Apologeticum* 39:7).
How can we give to God
what is God's?
By being converted
in every moment
to the new commandment,
not merely in word,
but in deed.
"This is *my* command"
(see Jn 13:34).
Then our conscience
can be at peace."[99]

At the foot of the cross
Mary became our Mother,
and like any good Mother
she desires that her children
love one another.
And that they love
as Jesus has loved them,
even to the point
of dying for them.[100]

"If I, your Lord and Teacher,
have washed your feet,
you also ought to
wash one another's feet" (Jn 13:14).
How shall we bring to life
this splendid Word
that proposes an unmatched
example of Christian love
given to us
by Jesus?
Christianity is love
and God requires
this service of love

from us.
But he doesn't ask this
only of individuals.
This Word clearly states
that it must be mutual:
"you also ought to wash
one another's feet."[101]

~

"As I have loved you" (see Jn 15:12).
That word "as"
in the new commandment
can be taken to mean
Jesus Forsaken,
not only readiness to give our
lives for each other,
but complete dying
for our brothers and sisters,
a stripping away, both within and
without, of all things spiritual
and material. This is a detachment
that generates unity.[102]

~

The basic rule
for being able
to pray
is unity
that is born
from mutual love.[103]

~

The Lord
has always urged us
to place,
at the basis of everything else,
mutual love.
There are many
who produce and produce,
with an activism
not entirely Christian.
"Above all,
maintain constant love for one another…"
(1 Pt 4:8).
Then your activities
will acquire value.[104]

~

With a fireplace
you must occasionally
pick up the poker and stir up the coals
so that the ashes don't bury them.
So too, every once in a while,
it is necessary to make a deliberate choice to
revive our mutual love,
to revive our relationships
so they are not covered
by ashes of apathy, indifference,
egoism…[105]

∼

Let's take advantage
of every opportunity
to allow the glowing white
flames of Love
to emanate from our hearts
and from the hearts of our
sisters and brothers.[106]

∼

Today,
let's try to live
the new commandment
and, with this as our only basis,
offer everything we do to Jesus,
repeating "For You, Jesus."
Pray always, yes,
but always grounded
in mutual love." [107]

~

"There am I
in the midst of them"
(see Mt 18:20).
Let's strive to never forget this,
or better still,
to never forget Jesus
who must come before
every other thing.
Jesus in our midst,
born of our mutual love,
is the great novelty
that we are called to offer
the world. What an honor

to have such a calling!
What perfect joy! [108]

∾

The cornerstone
of the spirituality
of communion
without doubt is
the new commandment. [109]

∾

You know,
unity
isn't accomplished
through mutual love
once and for all.
It has to be renewed
each day,
through thought
and action. [110]

∾

The new commandment
requires humility,
silencing self-love,
paying the price
of passing from
an individualistic way of living
to a communitarian spirituality.[111]

~

The Lord
will bless all our efforts
and, if we are faithful
to the new commandment,
he will give us the joy
of beholding his presence
among us, wherever we are.[112]

~

The new commandment
is the great opportunity
offered to us
for a more united world.[113]

The pact of mutual love
was the cornerstone
of our Movement.
It was where
Jesus came into our midst.
Let's try to renew it
and live accordingly.[114]

~

By living mutual love
the Risen Lord
will shine among us
with his Spirit,
as the Easter feast
requires.[115]

~

Jesus Forsaken
is the Divine Key
who makes it
truly possible
for us to be prepared
to give our lives
for each other.[116]

If you love,
you are often
loved in return.[117]

~

You know,
in the Trinity
they live love.
So Jesus brought
mutual love,
because this is how
the Persons
of the Most Holy Trinity
love.[118]

~

What a measure!
He died for us
and tells us that we should
love each other
to the point of
giving our lives
for each other.[119]

The followers of Jesus
cannot claim to be
genuine followers
unless they are capable
of giving their lives for
each other and for all.[120]

∼

We are not always asked
to give our lives.
Right now, for example,
you are merely listening
to my words: that's not
really giving your life.
But deep inside,
we should always be ready:
if I were asked to give my life,
I would give it. Deep inside,
deep inside…[121]

∼

We must first create
the necessary conditions,
the proper atmosphere
in which we can say to
one another:
"With the help of God's grace,
I want to be ready to give
my life for you." And then hear
the others respond: "And I am ready
to give my life for you." [122]

Mary is not a member
of the hierarchy,
but she is always
most active in the Church,
participating in its life
through the maternal love
in her heart,
— there where her sacrifice takes place —
sharing the sacrifice of her Son. [123]

Mary highlights
the Church's fundamental
aspect of love
that makes it "one"
as in the Trinity.
Thus she presents
to the world
the Bride of Christ
as Jesus desired her
and as all the people
today await her:
ordered love.[124]

Mary is the Mother
par excellence,
the prototype
of maternity and,
therefore, of love.
But since God is Love,
she appears as an
explanation of God,
an open book
that explains God.[125]

𝓛et's try
to love one another,
especially we Christians.
Doesn't Jesus warn
that even if we are about
to place our gift on the altar
and there recall that our
brother or sister
has something against us,
then it's better not to offer the gift?
First we should go
and be reconciled
with that brother or sister.
In Christianity,
mutual love is everything.[126]

𝒯he love in God
was so great
that it made Him
die for us,
in a most atrocious way.
All to save us!
Just

as the motive of a mother's love
is always the good of her child.
Since Mary is
the Mother Divine,
she is the creature
who most copies God,
who most reflects God.[127]

~

May we return to God
through Mary, and
because of her love
draw many
to return to her
heart, where they
will find God.
She will speak
the words of her Son
to us: "Blessed are
the pure in heart,
for they shall see God"
(Mt 5:8).
And we need
to see God
if we are to bring Him

into our relationships,
into our world.[128]

Who are we?
We're a
Movement of
men, women, and children
who, by loving one another,
try to live in such a way
as to have Jesus
spiritually in our midst.
What do we do, then?
We strive,
as Mary did,
to give Jesus
to the world.
This is where our strength
and beauty lie.
It's an invasion of love,
a true, beautiful
gospel love
among young and old.
So let us be proud
of our Mother,
the most beautiful and fascinating
Mother in the world![129]

"I give you a new commandment,
that you love one another.
Just as I have loved you,
you also should love one another" (Jn 13:34).
When two or more
live this Word,
Jesus is spiritually present
in their midst.
It can happen
in a factory, in a school,
in a family, anywhere.[130]

When we live
the new commandment,
living cells
of the Mystical Body
are born, and Christ
begins to reign
among two or more:
husband and wife,
employer and employee,
among colleagues at work,
among playmates
and friends.[131]

If the Mariapolis,
the city of Mary
had a motto,
it would have to be:
"And we have believed
in Mary's love."
Holding on
to this faith
and answering
to this love
we shall surely become
bearers of the Fire,
bearers of the Life,
which is Christ among us,
the Fruit of mutual love.[132]

Notes

1. Chiara Lubich Center Archives, "Meeting with Theology Students" (Berlin, July 7, 1960).
2. Chiara Lubich, *Nuova Umanità* 19 (1997/6) 114, 707.
3. Lubich, *La Via* 38 (November 12, 1949).
4. Chiara Lubich, *Essential Writings* (Hyde Park, NY: New City Press, 2007), 80.
5. Leonor Maria Salierno, *Maria negli scritti di Chiara Lubich* (Rome: Città Nuova, 1993), 192.
6. Salierno, *La Via*.
7. Ibid.
8. Chiara Lubich, *Essential Writings* (Hyde Park, NY: New City Press, 2007), 175.
9. Chiara Lubich and Igino Giordani, *Erano i tempi di guerra: Agli albori dell'ideale dell'unità* (Rome: Città Nuova, 2007), 14–24.
10. Chiara Lubich, "Questa è l'ora di S. Francesco, Il Natale di un'Idea," *L'amico serafico* (February 1948): 10.
11. Lubich and Giordani.
12. Ibid.
13. Ibid.
14. Ibid.
15. Ibid.
16. Ibid.

17. Ibid.
18. Ibid.
19. Ibid.
20. "Meeting with Theology Students."
21. Lubich, *La Via*.
22. Lubich and Giordani.
23. Lubich, *La Via*.
24. Lubich and Giordani.
25. Chiara Lubich Center Archives, "Meeting with Superiors General"(Villa Cavalletti, May 29, 1987).
26. Lubich and Giordani.
27. Lubich, *Tutti siano uno* (Rome: Città Nuova, 1968), 10–11.
28. Lubich and Giordani.
29. Chiara Lubich Center Archives, "Meeting with Youth" (Santiago di Campostela, August 17, 1989).
30. Chiara Lubich Center Archives, "Meeting with Seminarians" (Rome, May 22, 2001).
31. Lubich, *A New Way* (Hyde Park, NY: New City Press, 2006), 50.
32. Lubich, *Cercando le cose di lassù* (Rome: Città Nuova, 1992), 137–138.
33. Lubich, *Santi insieme* (Rome: Città Nuova, 1994), 95–96.
34. Ibid.
35. Gen's 20 (1990), 81, 83.

36. Chiara Lubich, *E Torna Natale* (Rome: Città Nuova, 1997), 49.
37. Lubich, *Santi insieme*.
38. Gen's 20.
39. Lubich and Giordani.
40. Lubich, "Questa è l'ora di S. Francesco, Il Natale di un'Idea," *L'amico serafico* (February 1948): 12.
41. Ibid.
42. Lubich, *Santi insieme*.
43. Lubich and Giordani.
44. Chiara Lubich Center Archives (unpublished). See also *Rivista Gen* XXIII (1989): 8–10.
45. Lubich and Giordani.
46. Lubich. *Gesù nel fratello* (Rome: Città Nuova, 1979), 103–104.
47. Lubich and Giordani.
48. Ibid.
49. Lubich, *Cercando le cose di lassù*.
50. Lubich, *E Torna Natale*, 24
51. Lubich and Giordani.
52. Ibid.
53. Lubich, *Gesù nel fratello*.
54. Lubich, *La Via*.
55. Lubich, *Gesù nel fratello*.
56. Lubich, *La vita, un viaggio* (Rome: Città Nuova, 1985), 146–147.
57. Ibid.

58. Ibid.
59. Ibid.
60. Ibid.
61. Chiara Lubich Center Archives, "Diary of Chiara Lubich" (April 11, 1968).
62. Ibid.
63. Chiara Lubich Center Archives, "Diary of Chiara Lubich" (March 27, 1970).
64. Chiara Lubich Center Archives, "Meeting with European Zone directors" (Rome, April 11, 1974).
65. Ibid.
66. Ibid.
67. Chiara Lubich Center Archives, "Meeting with priests and religious" (Loppiano June 26, 1969).
68. Ibid.
69. Ibid.
70. Ibid.
71. Ibid.
72. Ibid.
73. Ibid.
74. Ibid.
75. Ibid.
76. Ibid.
77. Ibid.
78. Chiara Lubich Center Archives, "Diary of Chiara Lubich" (October 26, 1980).
79. Chiara Lubich Center Archives, "Conference Call" (August 25, 1994).

80. Lubich, *La Via*.
81. Chiara Lubich Center Archives, "Diary of Chiara Lubich" (October 26, 1980).
82. Ibid.
83. Chiara Lubich Center Archives, "Meeting with a group of bishops" (Istanbul, October 9, 1984).
84. Ibid.
85. Chiara Lubich Center Archives, "Conference Call" (June 8, 1989).
86. Lubich, "Dio lo vuole," *L'Amico serafico* (March-April 1947).
87. Chiara Lubich Center Archives, "Meeting with Theology Students" (Berlin, July 7, 1960).
88. Lubich, *A New Way*, 50.
89. Chiara Lubich Center Archives, "Meeting with religious" (Castel Gandolfo, May 13, 1988).
90. Ibid.
91. Lubich, *Essential Writings*, 205.
92. Chiara Lubich Center Archives (Rocca di Papa October 5, 1978).
93. Lubich, *Essential Writings*, 205.
94. Chiara Lubich Center Archives, "Meeting with zone directors" (Rocca di Papa, November 5, 1995).
95. Ibid.
96. Lubich, *Essential Writings*, p. 205.
97. Chiara Lubich Center Archives (Loppiano, April 18, 2000).

98. Chiara Lubich Center Archives, "Meeting with bishops," (February 12, 1980).
99. Chiara Lubich Center Archives, "Meeting with youth" (Rome, April 12, 1984).
100. Salierno, *Maria negli scritti di Chiara Lubich*.
101. Chiara Lubich Center Archives, "Conference Call" (April 1, 1982).
102. Chiara Lubich, *La vita, un viaggio* (Rome: Città Nuova, 1984), 39–41.
103. Chiara Lubich, *Santità di popolo* (Rome: Città Nuova, 2001), 76–77.
104. Chiara Lubich, *Costruendo il castello esteriore* (Rome: Città Nuova, 2002), 71–72.
105. Chiara Lubich, *Cercando le cose di lassù* (Rome: Città Nuova, 1992), 96–97.
106. Ibid.
107. Ibid.
108. Lubich, *Costruendo il castello esteriore*.
109. Ibid.
110. Lubich, *Santità di popolo*, 22–23.
111. Ibid.
112. Ibid.
113. Ibid.
114. Lubich, *Santi insieme*, 26–27.
115. Ibid.
116. Ibid.
117. Ibid.
118. Insert, *Rivista Gen* XXIII (1989): 8–10.

119. Ibid.
120. Ibid.
121. Ibid.
122. Ibid.
123. Salierno, 88.
124. Ibid., 89.
125. Ibid., 99.
126. Ibid., 193.
127. Ibid., 99.
128. Ibid., 108
129. Ibid., 112.
130. Ibid., 136.
131. Ibid.
132. Ibid., 146.

NEW CITY PRESS
of the Focolare

Hyde Park, New York

About New City Press of the Focolare

New City Press is one of more than 20 publishing houses sponsored by the Focolare, a movement founded by Chiara Lubich to help bring about the realization of Jesus' prayer: "That all may be one" (John 17:21). In view of that goal, New City Press publishes books and resources that enrich the lives of people and help all to strive toward the unity of the entire human family. We are a member of the Association of Catholic Publishers.

Further Reading

5 Steps to Living Christian Unity	978-1-56548-485-5	$ 4.95
15 Days of Prayer with Dorothy Day	978-1-56548-491-7	$11.95
Gospel in Action	978-1-56548-486-3	$12.95
A New Way	978-1-56548-236-4	$12.95
Walking Together	978-1-56548-526-6	$19.00

Coming Soon

5 Steps to Facing Suffering	978-1-56548-502-0	$ 4.95
Polly's Little Kite	978-1-56548-528-0	$11.95

Periodicals
Living City Magazine,

www.livingcitymagazine.com

Scan to join our mailing list for discounts and promotions or go to www.newcitypress.com and click on "join our email list."